0

A TASTE OF INDIA

Roz Denny

Wayland

Titles in this series

A TASTE OF

Britain	Italy
The Caribbean	Japan
China	Mexico
France	Spain
India	West Africa

Cover *The beautiful Taj Mahal palace is one of India's most famous landmarks.*

Frontispiece *Indians love snacks. These ones are made from rice, potatoes and chickpeas.*

Editor: Anna Girling
Designer: Jean Wheeler

First published in 1994 by
Wayland (Publishers) Ltd
61 Western Road, Hove
East Sussex, BN3 1JD, England

© Copyright 1994 Wayland (Publishers) Ltd

British Library Cataloguing in Publication Data
Denny, Roz
Taste of India. – (Food Around the World Series)
I. Title II. Series
641.300954

ISBN 0 7502 0796 5

Typeset by Dorchester Typesetting Group Ltd
Printed and bound by Lego, Italy

Contents

India in the world today   4

The history of Indian food   9

Food from the regions   12

Farming and crops   14

Cooking and eating in India   19

Spices and curries   23

Other everyday foods   26

Festival food   32

Kitchiri   34

Naan   36

Vermicelli pudding   38

Tandoori chicken drumsticks   40

Lamb and *basmati pillau*   42

Raita   44

Glossary   45

Further information   47

Index   48

India in the world today

India is an important country in the world today. Through its people and culture, its influence has reached many other parts of the world.

India is a very densely populated country. It is one-third the size of the USA, yet it has about three times the population – more than 850 million. There are also about another 17 million Indians living in other parts of the world, including Britain, the Middle East, Africa and North America.

India is a very crowded country – and a very colourful one.

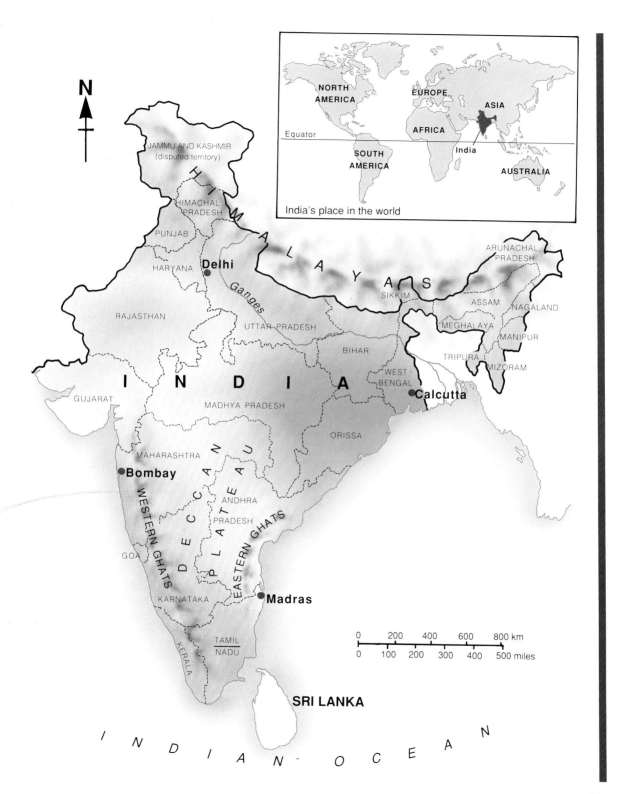

N

JAMMU AND KASHMIR
(disputed territory)

HIMACHAL
PRADESH

PUNJAB

HARYANA

Delhi

RAJASTHAN

Ganges

UTTAR PRADESH

HIMALAYAS

ARUNACHAL
PRADESH

SIKKIM

ASSAM

NAGALAND

MEGHALAYA

MANIPUR

BIHAR

TRIPURA

MIZORAM

WEST
BENGAL

Calcutta

GUJARAT

I N D I A

MADHYA PRADESH

ORISSA

MAHARASHTRA

Bombay

ANDHRA
PRADESH

WESTERN GHATS

DECCAN PLATEAU

EASTERN GHATS

GOA

KARNATAKA

Madras

TAMIL
NADU

KERALA

SRI LANKA

I N D I A N   O C E A N

India's place in the world

NORTH
AMERICA

EUROPE

ASIA

Equator

AFRICA

India

SOUTH
AMERICA

AUSTRALIA

| 0 | 200 | 400 | 600 | 800 km |
| 0 | 100 | 200 | 300 | 400 | 500 miles |

A taste of India

In India there are:
- 25 states and seven territories
- 16 main languages (including English)
- six main religious groups (including Hindus, Muslims, Christians and Sikhs)

With so many different people, no wonder the food of India is so varied and delicious!

Indians are extremely proud of their culture. Although many now live according to Western ways, Indians value their history and pass on their traditions to their children.

The land

Geographers call India a subcontinent because it is so large. It covers an area of more than 3 million square kilometres. In fact it is almost big enough to be a continent in itself, like Europe.

India is a long, pointed land mass, or peninsular, sticking out from the rest of southern Asia. It is bordered to the east and west by seas, and to the north by the largest mountain range in the world – the Himalayas. It has every type of landscape.

A Himalayan landscape in northern India.

In the north are snowy mountains. South of the mountains are thickly wooded foothills and fertile valleys. These in turn give way to a vast, flat plain, containing one of India's great rivers, the Ganges. This plain is the centre of Indian culture. Today it is a densely populated area with many big cities, including Delhi, India's capital, and Calcutta.

Southern India juts out into the Indian Ocean. In the centre is a high, flat land area called the Deccan Plateau, with two mountain ranges on either side – the Eastern and Western Ghats. All round are coastal plains. Two other big cities are in southern India – Bombay and Madras. (The large island of Sri Lanka, off the tip of India, is a separate country.)

Above *South of the Himalayas are foothills and green valleys.*
Below *The Thar Desert is very dry. Camels are used because they need very little water.*

Climate

Generally speaking, India is a very hot country. It includes some of the hottest places in the world, with temperatures of up to 40° C. In the north, the climate is temperate, with cold winters, warm summers and a high rainfall.

On the vast northern plain, the summers are very hot and the winters mild. For much of the year there is very little rain and occasionally there are even dust storms.

Above *Palm trees grow in the tropical coastal areas of southern India.*
Below *The monsoon brings heavy rain.*

The Deccan Plateau is dry too, but the coastal plains around it have a lot of rain. In these parts, tropical plants grow.

There are three seasons in India. Cool and dry, hot and dry and very rainy. This last season is the time of the monsoon winds, which last from June to September. Heavy monsoon rains bring welcome relief from the great heat, plus much-needed water for crops. But the monsoon can also bring flooding and storms, called typhoons, which can cause havoc and kill many people. In some years, the monsoon brings too little rain, and crops die.

The history of Indian food

In India, many dishes and recipes date from ancient times. Over 4,000 years ago, one of the world's great ancient civilizations grew up around the River Indus, to the north-west of India. These ancient people learnt to control the river's water with dams and canals. They built towns and temples and started to grow crops. Later, various armies of warriors invaded and took control.

One group of these invaders, the Aryans, settled down and continued to develop civilization. They grew crops, such as wheat, barley and rice, because they were able to control water supplies. They also introduced a language called Sanskrit which became the language of the Hindu religion.

In about AD 1000 yet another wave of warriors invaded from the north-west. They brought a new religion, the Muslim religion of Islam. The descendants of these invaders were known as Moguls. They formed an important empire that brought great culture to India. They encouraged art, literature and music.

Above *This carving, found near the River Indus, is about 4,000 years old.*
Below *A picture of the great Moghul emperor, Akbar.*

The beautiful Taj Mahal was built in the seventeenth century by a Moghul emperor in memory of his wife, after her death.

The Moguls also developed delicious recipes and some of India's most famous dishes date from this time.

Food and religion

Millions of Indians are vegetarians because it is against their religion to eat meat. They have delicious ways of cooking lentils, dairy products, vegetables, breads and rice. Some religions will not even allow the eating of onions, root vegetables like carrots, and tomatoes.

Over three-quarters of Indians are Hindus. Most Hindus are vegetarians and all Hindus believe cows are sacred animals. So Hindus do not eat beef at all, although foods can be made from cows' milk, including yogurt, cheese and a cooked butter fat called *ghee*.

A tenth of Indians are Muslims, who are not allowed to eat pork. Most of the meat dishes in India use just mutton (or lamb) and chicken.

Foods from America

In 1499, seven years after Christopher Columbus first sailed from Europe to America, a Portuguese explorer called Vasco da Gama returned home from India with a shipload of exotic spices. In return, the Portuguese introduced the hot chilli pepper from the Americas to Indians. Up to then, although Indians had used aromatic spices, their food had not been spicy hot. Other foods from America, such as tomatoes and potatoes, also became popular with Indian cooks.

Hot chilli peppers left to dry.

The British in India

In the seventeenth century the British set up a trading company in India, known as the East India Company. Eventually, this led to Britain controlling all of India.

The system of British rule in India became known as the British Raj. Many popular British dishes today are based on Indian recipes, such as chutney, curry, kedgeree and rice pudding. Now, the joy of Indian food has spread around the world, with many restaurants serving delicious, spiced dishes.

Kedgeree is a British dish of rice, fish, egg and, usually, curry powder.

Food from the regions

The dishes that India is most famous for – the ones now eaten in restaurants around the world – come from different regions of the country. For example, *tikka* and *tandoori* were developed by warriors from Rajasthan in north-west India. They grilled their pieces of meat on skewers to make *tikka* (or maybe the warriors used their swords), after marinating it first with spices and oil or yogurt. Larger pieces of meat would be roasted in a special clay-lined oven called a *tandoor* – hence *tandoori* meat.

A tandoor *is an oven lined with clay. This one is being used to cook* naan *bread.*

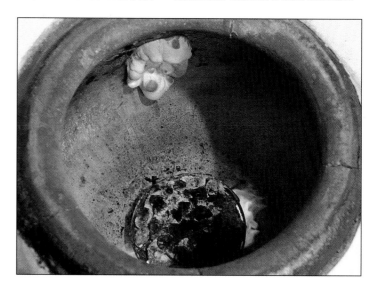

Locally caught fish is used in many dishes in southern India.

Next to Rajasthan is the state of Gujarat, which is famous for its vegetarian dishes. Gujaratis use many types of pulses, lentils, vegetables, breads, rice, yogurt, eggs and a cheese called *paneer*.

In southern India, rice is very popular. Fish is also eaten a lot around the coast. Many meat dishes come from the Muslim state of Andhra Pradesh: there is *korma* (a creamy, mildly spiced meat dish) and *biriyani*, a rich dish of rice and meat often cooked at festivals.

One of India's hottest dishes – *vindaloo* – contains plenty of fiery chillies and is often cooked with pork. It comes from the Christian area of Goa, on the west coast, where the Portuguese settled many centuries ago.

Farming and crops

Farmers all over India use cattle to pull their ploughs. In the background of this picture is a field of sugar-cane.

Irrigation (watering the land) is important in dry areas. This village uses water from a well to irrigate the land and produce more crops.

Nearly three-quarters of Indians are farmers and most of them own very small areas of land – barely enough to grow food for one family. Many villages are still without proper drainage, electricity and modern tools. Unless farming methods are improved, there will not be enough food to feed India's growing population. In some villages, the people have joined together to form co-operatives, or groups that help each other to farm the land. In these places life has improved. However, poverty is still a great problem in India and diseases and hunger remain.

A family of Indian peasant farmers all works together. The mother gets up first to clean the house and prepare a simple breakfast. Then the father goes into the fields by 6 am, and works in the great heat with only a short break at lunch time. At busy periods, children also help in the fields after school.

The main food crops in India are rice, wheat, sugar-cane and pulses. Tea is also grown and is exported to other countries.

Rice

India is the world's second largest grower of rice, after China. The average Indian eats about 200 g of rice a day — that is about 73 kg a year! In the United Kingdom the average is 3 kg a year.

This girl is helping her mother to plant out crops. Many children help in the fields after school.

Rice seedlings are planted out in flooded paddy fields.

A taste of India

Growing rice involves several stages. The seeds are sown and grown into seedlings. Then, the young rice seedlings are replanted by hand in paddy fields which have been flooded with water to stop attacks by insects.

There are many varieties of rice grown in India. The most popular are long-grain rices. A very high-quality rice, *basmati*, is grown in the foothills of the Himalayas and is expensive because it grows quite slowly. *Basmati* smells delicious – the name means 'the fragrant one' in Hindi.

Cook your own perfect rice

Ingredients
Serves 4

250g long-grain rice (not the easy-cook type)
2 tablespoons cooking oil
1 teaspoon salt
600 ml water

Cooked basmati *rice.*

16

Equipment

sieve
large saucepan
wooden spoon
fork

3 Pour in the water, add the salt and bring to the boil. Cover with a lid, then lower the heat to a gentle simmer. Cook for 12 minutes. No peeking, or you will let out the steam!

1 Rinse the rice in a sieve under cold running water. Drain well.

4 Remove the pan from the heat with the lid still on. Leave for 5 minutes, then uncover and stir with a fork.

2 Heat the oil in the saucepan and fry the rice, stirring with a wooden spoon, for about a minute.

Always be careful with boiling liquid. Ask an adult to help you.

A taste of India

Tea leaves are picked by hand by women.

Indian tea is not like the tea drunk in Western countries. It is boiled up in a pan.

Tea

The northern hilly regions of Assam and Darjeeling have some of the highest rainfall in the world, sometimes up to 190 cm a year. This is ideal for growing tea. Tea, called *chay* in India, is drunk all over the country and great amounts are exported around the world.

Tea is grown in plantations. The tea leaves are picked by hand by women. Only the very tips are picked. It is extremely hard work.

Much of the tea from Assam ends up in our tea-bags. Darjeeling tea is a higher quality and most of it is still sold as leaves to be brewed in the traditional way using a pot and strainer.

Chay (Indian tea) is made by boiling water, milk, sugar and spices with tea leaves, then straining it into small cups.

Cooking and eating in India

Some Indians have kitchens similar to those in the West. But many millions of people cook over one burner, often out of doors. The fuel might be wood, charcoal or cow dung mixed with straw and baked in the sun until it is hard. Some people might have a gas burner. Cooking is usually done in batches. The food is reheated quickly before serving if necessary.

An outdoor kitchen in northern India. Many people cook outdoors.

Idlis *(steamed rice cakes)* are eaten for breakfast.

A meal may consist of rice, vegetables and meat or lentils.

Meal times

Indians like to eat three good hot meals a day. Breakfast is often reheated spiced rice and breads left over from the day before. In southern India, breakfast might consist of steamed rice cakes, called *idlis*, or rice pancakes called *dosa*. Sometimes *chapatis* are cut into pieces, fried in spicy oil and mixed to a porridge with yogurt, garlic and spices.

Lunch is a full meal with rice, breads, cooked vegetables, *raitas* (chopped or grated raw vegetables, such as cucumber or beetroot, with yogurt) and a main dish of lentils or meat.

Children and adults who work away from the home will have their lunch served to them in 'tiffin' boxes. These are round metal food containers, stacked on top of each other, with carrying handles. At about 11 am each day, special 'tiffin-carriers' called *dabba wallahs* will collect tiffin boxes from people's houses and take them to offices or schools so that members of the family can eat their lunch.

The evening meal is yet another delicious home-cooked meal. All meals in India are served with lots of pickles, relishes and *raitas.*

A man carrying a tiffin box at lunchtime.

Snack food

The railways of India are world famous. Many people travel long distances on them. At every station, and inside the trains too, food and drink sellers offer delicious snacks and sweet treats. When you stop at a station, food sellers knock at your window and offer you snacks and *chay* in small cups.

Indians also enjoy little snacks during the day. Most popular are *poppadums*, thin rounds of bread made with lentil flour and dried in the sun. They go crispy when grilled on an open fire.

21

A taste of India

Samosas

Other popular snacks include *samosas*. These are little triangles of fried, wafer-thin pastry wrapped around spicy fillings of vegetables, pulses or meat.

Eating in India – using one hand and a chapati.

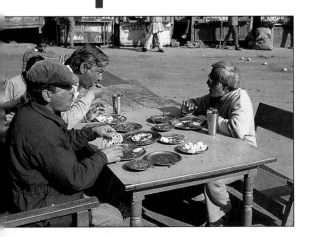

How to eat Indian-style

While many city people might use knives and forks to eat with, most Indians still use their fingers because they like to feel the lovely texture of their food. There is quite a knack to doing it neatly! Here are some tips:

● Always use your right hand. It is bad manners to use your left hand. Wash both hands very well before you begin.
● Tear off a piece of *chapati*, about the size of half a small saucer.
● Fold it to form a scoop and shovel up the food from a plate, then pop it into your mouth.
● Remember, you can only use one hand to tear, fold and scoop, so keep practising!

Spices and curries

The word 'curry' is an English term used to describe the spicy stews eaten by Indians. The word is thought to come from the south of India, where a people called the Tamils live. The Tamils call their spicy sauces '*kari*'. The word 'curry' is not used by Indians.

Spices are so important in all Indian food that is hard to imagine a meal without them. They give a delicious, aromatic flavour to even the simplest of foods. Children in India are not fussy eaters and love the lightly spiced sauces, fragrant, fresh, flat breads, rice and vegetables India is well known for. Very young children do not eat highly spiced foods, but most Indians grow up with spices.

Bags of spices for sale at a city market.

A taste of India

A basket of crocus flowers which will be used to make saffron.

Chilli peppers give Indian food its hot spiciness.

The main spices used in India

Cumin Small, long, thin seeds which are ground up to make a powder.

Coriander Small, pale-brown, round, dried berries. The leaves, too, are used – in the same way as parsley.

Asafoetida A strong, bitter powder used to bring out the flavour of food.

Fenugreek Small, pale-yellow, square-shaped seeds.

Ginger A hot-tasting root. It is used fresh (grated or chopped) or dried (as a powder).

Cinnamon Long, thin pieces of rolled tree bark.

Cloves Dried, unopened flower buds from the clove tree. They have a very strong taste if you bite them.

Cardamom Pods with green outer casings and small, aromatic black seeds inside.

Chillies Fresh green or dried red chillies are used. They are spicy hot and should be used carefully because they can cause stinging. After cutting them, be careful not to rub your eyes.

Fennel Small seeds with an aniseed flavour like liquorice.

Garam masala A mixture of spices all ground together. Cooks often make their own blend.

Turmeric When fresh, this is a root like ginger, but it is often sold dried and ground into a powder. It turns food a bright yellow colour.

Mustard seeds and **poppy seeds** Small, black, round seeds. They pop when heated in a pan.

Saffron Probably the world's most expensive spice, saffron is used only for special dishes. It comes from a particular crocus and turns food yellow.

Cooking with spices

Most Indians buy spices whole and grind them to a powder using a pestle and mortar. The spices are stored in small, round tins contained in another, larger, round tin.

Spices are always best lightly heated before grinding. This brings out the fullest flavour. When they are used, the ground spices are fried briefly in hot oil to bring out more flavour before the rest of the cooking is continued.

This woman is sorting coriander seeds.

Three forms of cinnamon: (from top) the bark; rolled into sticks; ground into powder.

Other everyday foods

Indian breads

Bread is very important in India. It is eaten at every meal and there is a great variety of delicious types. Most of it is unleavened. This means it is not made to rise with yeast, like the sliced bread used in the West for sandwiches or toast. Instead it remains flat.

The most common breads are *chapatis* and the slightly richer *parathas*, which can be stuffed with vegetables and minced meat. Small balls of dough are rolled out into thin rounds, then cooked

Making chapatis. Small balls of dough are rolled out and cooked on a hot metal plate.

Puffy purees *are deep fried in hot oil.*

quickly on heavy, metal hotplates called *tavas*. It takes a long time to learn to roll the dough with one hand while you flip the cooked bread with the other – even more difficult when you have to squat over an open wood or charcoal fire, fanning it occasionally to keep the flames going!

Other breads, called *purees*, are small and puffy. They are deep fried in hot oil in a pan which looks like a Chinese *wok*. Little rounds of dough are slipped carefully into the oil and puff up almost instantly.

Naan breads are made from dough leavened with yeast. This causes them to rise a little.

27

A taste of India

Vegetables for sale at a market. How many can you recognize? Are there any you do not know?

A dish of spicy okra.

Vegetables

Because India has so many vegetarians, there are many wonderful vegetables and recipes for cooking them. Here are some popular vegetables.

Aubergines Long and thick with shiny purple skins. When cooked, they go soft and creamy.

Spinach Green, leafy and very nutritious. In India it is often fried with spices.

Okra (sometimes known as ladies' fingers) Long and green with small seeds inside. Okra is used a lot in stews.

Potatoes Very popular, especially in vegetarian dishes.

Cauliflower Again, very popular and often cooked with whole spices.

Indians also use other vegetables eaten all over the world, such as peas, peppers, beans, cabbage, tomatoes, carrots and mushrooms. Almost all vegetables are cooked in delicious ways, using spices, onions, garlic, ginger and coconut cream.

Pulses

Pulses are very healthy foods because they contain a lot of proteins. Proteins are the substances in food that help us to grow and keep our strength up. Meat is an excellent source of protein, but because most Indians are vegetarians they have to get their protein from vegetable foods such as pulses.

Neat piles of pulses on sale at a street stall. Look at the different shapes and colours.

A taste of India

Lentils are cooked with spices to make a kind of runny stew.

There are lentils and split peas (both of which Indians call *dhal*) and dried beans. When cooked, pulses can either be creamy or have a good firm texture. Here are some of the most popular ones.

Masoor dhal A type of lentil with a brown skin and orangy-yellow inside.

Green lentils Flat, greeny-brown, disc-shaped lentils.

Chickpeas, red kidney beans and **aduki beans** Firm beans that hold their shape well when cooked.

Drinks

There are lots of popular drinks in India. In towns and cities you will find many street stalls selling drinks as a quick refreshment. Spiced tea (called *masal chay*) is made by boiling milk, water and sugar with tea leaves and spices such as cloves, cinnamon and cardamom.

Lassi is a refreshing, cool yogurt drink made of yogurt curd mixed with water, salt or sugar and sometimes mint.

India grows a lot of sugar-cane. When the stalks are crushed, the sweet juice is mixed with fresh lime juice or fresh ginger to make a refreshing drink.

However, as in the rest of the world, fizzy, sweet, cola-type drinks are also popular in India.

A drink stall in Bombay selling fresh fruit juices as well as bottled fizzy drinks.

Sweets and desserts

Indians love sweet foods, which they usually serve at the end of a meal or as snacks. Sweet, thick *purees*, called *halvas*, are very popular. These are made from carrots or semolina, flavoured with spices such as cardamom, and have almonds, pistachio nuts or sultanas stirred in.

Traditional Indian sweets: the yellow square (centre) is a halva; *the yellow balls are called* ladu *and are eaten at weddings; the rest are sweets made from milk, with nuts or spices added.*

Light, milk puddings, called *kheer*, are made with rice or *vermicelli* and often flavoured with rose-water.

Indian ice-cream, called *kulfi*, is very rich and comes in flavours such as mango or pistachio.

31

Festival food

Indians love to celebrate, whether it is a wedding or a religious festival. Some celebrations can go on for days and food plays an important part.

At weddings, rice and rose petals are thrown over the happy couple for good luck. This is where the Western custom for throwing rice and confetti comes from. No matter what the religion of the people involved, an important part of an Indian wedding is the sweet dish served during the meal. Although it is a sweet,

These delicious-looking dishes were prepared for a wedding and kept in large pots until the guests were ready to eat.

At the festival of Diwali, Hindus light lamps or candles.

it is actually the main dish and is the middle course. Many different types of sweet may be served. Some of the most popular are made from semolina dough fried in hot *ghee*, sweetened with sugar or syrup.

The most important religious festival for Hindus is called *Diwali*, the festival of lights. It is a magical time when streets, homes and public buildings are all lit up. Friends exchange sweets, nuts and fruits. There are fireworks and fairs. Because it is a Hindu festival no meat is served, but all the food is made in rich, special ways, using lots of spices, butter and nuts. Sweets and desserts have wafer-thin layers of real silver leaf placed on top. Even the silver can be eaten.

The most important Muslim festival is *Id*, which marks the end of the month of *Ramadan*. During *Ramadan* Muslims over the age of twelve fast, which means they do not eat or drink during daylight hours. Muslims celebrate *Id* with delicious spicy meat dishes and sweets.

This procession in Bombay is being held to celebrate the Muslim festival of Id.

Kitchiri

Ingredients
Serves 4-6

250 g long-grain rice
1 onion, peeled
1 small green pepper
1 clove garlic, peeled
25 g butter or
   margarine
1 tablespoon oil
1 teaspoon ground
   turmeric
1 teaspoon ground
   coriander
$1/2$ teaspoon ground
   cumin
430 g can green
   continental lentils,
   drained
2 tablespoons fresh
   chopped parsley or
   coriander
salt and ground black
   pepper

The British breakfast dish, kedgeree, is supposed to have developed from this Indian recipe. *Kitchiri* is a very healthy and tasty dish.

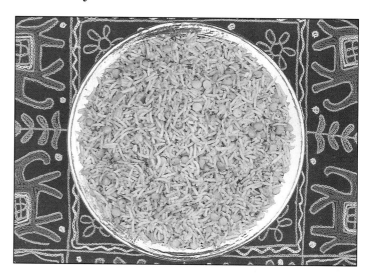

Kitchiri *is a combination of rice and pulses.*

Equipment

1 medium saucepan   can-opener
1 large saucepan   garlic crusher
knife   wooden spoon
chopping board   serving dish

Always be careful with hot oil and boiling liquid. Ask an adult to help you.

1 Boil the rice according to the instructions on pages 16-17 and keep it warm.

2 Chop the onion quite finely. Cut the pepper in half, remove the seeds and core, then chop to the same size as the onion. Crush the garlic in a garlic crusher.

3 In a large saucepan, melt the butter with the oil and gently fry the onion, pepper and garlic for about 5 minutes until softened.

4 Stir in the spices and cook for 1 minute. Then add 450 ml water and the lentils. Bring to the boil, then add a little salt and pepper.

5 Simmer for 10 minutes, stirring once or twice, then mix in the rice. Cook for 3 more minutes. Serve hot, spooned out on to a serving dish, sprinkled with the fresh chopped parsley or coriander.

Naan

Ingredients
Makes 8 breads

500 g strong white flour
1 sachet easy-blend
    dried yeast
2 teaspoons salt
1 teaspoon cumin seeds
1 tablespoon sesame
    or poppy seeds
150 g natural yogurt
200 ml warm water
25 g butter, melted
a little extra flour, for
    rolling
a little oil, for cooking

Equipment

large bowl
sieve
wooden spoon
wooden board
cling film
rolling pin
griddle pan or heavy-
    based frying pan
cup and pastry brush
tea towel

This is a leavened bread, made with yeast.

Naan *breads*.

1 Sift the flour into a big bowl. Add the yeast and salt and stir in the seeds.

2   Mix the yogurt, water and butter together and stir into the flour with a big wooden spoon.

3   With clean hands, tip the dough out on to a board. Rub the dough hard as if you were scrubbing clothes. This is called kneading and makes the dough nice and smooth. Do this for at least 5 minutes.

4   Put the dough back in the bowl, cover with cling film and leave to rise in a warm part of the kitchen until it has doubled in size. This will take between 2 and 4 hours, depending on the warmth of the room.

Always be careful with hot oil and pans. Ask an adult to help you.

5   Punch the dough so that it collapses. Take it out of the bowl and knead it again for 1 minute. Cut it into 8 equal pieces and roll each to a ball.

6   Sprinkle a little flour on a work surface and roll each ball out to an oval shape (the Indians say 'like a tear drop').

7   Heat a griddle pan or heavy-based frying pan until quite hot, brush it lightly with some oil and cook each bread for about 3 minutes on each side. Watch that it does not burn. Keep the breads warm, wrapped in a clean tea towel, while you make the rest.

Vermicelli *pudding*

Ingredients
Serves 4-6

75 g *vermicelli* pasta,
    broken up a little
3 tablespoons sugar
5 cardamoms
2 bay leaves
900 ml milk
2-3 tablespoons
    sultanas
2 tablespoons flaked
    almonds
170 g can evaporated
    milk
freshly grated nutmeg,
    if liked

Equipment

large saucepan
wooden spoon
can-opener
pretty serving bowl

Use very thin *spaghetti*, called *vermicelli*, for this quick milk pudding.

Kheer *is an Indian milk pudding made with rice, similar to this* vermicelli *recipe.*

Always be careful with boiling liquid. Ask an adult to help you.

1 Crush the *vermicelli* into a large saucepan. Add the sugar.

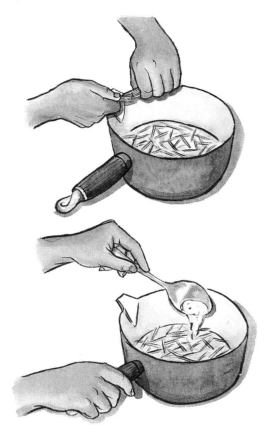

2 Split open the cardamom pods and scrape the small black seeds into the pan. Throw away the outer shells.

3 Add the bay leaves and milk. Bring to the boil, stirring occasionally. Watch it does not boil over, then turn the heat down.

4 Simmer the pudding, stirring 2 or 3 times, for 15 minutes.

5 Mix in the sultanas, almonds and evaporated milk. Cool and serve in a pretty glass bowl. If you like, sprinkle the top with some nutmeg.

Tandoori *chicken* *drumsticks*

Pieces of chicken cooked tandoori-*style.*

You can use a ready-made Indian *tandoori* paste from a shop for this. These pastes are excellent and taste just like home-made ones.

Ingredients
Serves 3-6

6 chicken drumsticks
1 tablespoon *tandoori* paste

150 g natural yogurt
1 teaspoon sea salt
1 lemon
sprigs of fresh parsley or coriander, to garnish

Equipment

small bowl
polythene food bag
baking sheet
knife and chopping
board
serving dish

1 Pull the skin off the chicken and throw it away.

2 Mix the *tandoori* paste with the yogurt and salt in a bowl, then spoon it into the food bag.

Always be careful with a hot oven. Ask an adult to help you.

3 Pop the chicken pieces into the bag, tie the top up, then rub the paste well into the chicken. Leave in the fridge for 30 minutes while you heat the oven to 180°C, 350°F, gas mark 4.

4 Remove the chicken from the bag (do not worry if it is rather messy) and place on a baking sheet. Cook in the oven for about 25 to 30 minutes.

5 Cut the lemon into 8 wedges. Arrange the chicken on a serving plate and garnish with the lemon and fresh sprigs of parsley or coriander. Serve with bread, such as the *naan* recipe on page 36, and *raita* (see page 44).

Lamb and basmati *pillau*

This is a rich rice dish, ideal for serving on special occasions, such as a party or to celebrate a festival like *Diwali.* You can leave out the saffron as it is expensive, but it *is* delicious! You can also use beef instead of lamb – but not for Hindus.

Always be careful with hot oil and boiling liquid. Ask an adult to help you.

Ingredients
Serves 4-6

a small piece of fresh
   root ginger, about
   2 cm long
2 cloves garlic, peeled
1 teaspoon ground
   turmeric
2 tablespoons oil
saffron strands to fill
   a small teaspoon, if
   liked
500 g lean minced
   lamb (or beef)
1 large onion, peeled
   and sliced
250 g *basmati* rice
600 ml water
4 cardamom pods
2 tablespoons fresh,
   chopped coriander
   or parsley
1 small lemon, juice
   only
25 g butter or *ghee*
salt and pepper
2 tablespoons
   pistachio nuts or
   flaked almonds

Equipment

grater
garlic crusher
large saucepan
   with lid
wooden spoon
small bowl
knife
chopping board
sieve
cup
lemon squeezer

1   Peel the ginger thinly and grate it. Crush the garlic and, in a small bowl, mix it with the ginger, turmeric and half the oil to make a paste.

2   Soak the saffron strands in a cup with two tablespoons of hot water and set aside.

3   Heat the remaining oil in the saucepan and fry the meat until well browned, stirring with a wooden spoon. Add the ginger paste and continue frying for 1 minute.

4   Stir in the onion and cook for another 2 minutes.

5   Add the *basmati*, saffron strands with their soaking water, the 600 ml of water and the cardamom pods. Cook for a minute and stir again. Add 1 teaspoon of salt, bring to the boil, then turn down the heat to a simmer and cover.

6   Cook for 10 minutes. Remove from the heat and, without lifting the lid, leave for 5 minutes.

7   Uncover, remove the cardamom pods which will have floated to the top, then stir in the chopped coriander or parsley, lemon juice and butter or *ghee*. Season with salt and pepper and serve hot, sprinkled with the nuts.

Raita

Raita.

Ingredients
Serves 4

$^1/_2$ cucumber
$^1/_2$ small onion, peeled
250 g thick natural yogurt
2 tablespoons fresh
   chopped mint
$^1/_2$ teaspoon cumin seeds
sea salt and ground
   black pepper

Equipment

grater
medium-sized bowl
wooden spoon
serving dish

Serve this with main course dishes.

1 Grate the cucumber on the biggest holes of the grater and place it in a bowl. Grate in the onion. You do not need much.

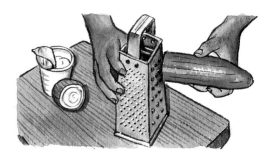

2 Mix in the yogurt, mint, cumin seeds and some salt and pepper. Spoon into a serving bowl and chill in the fridge until you eat.

Glossary

Ancient civilization A society, or group of people, that developed thousands of years ago. The ancient civilizations of the world set up amazingly organized systems of law, farming, building and the arts. They include the ancient Greeks, ancient Romans and ancient Egyptians.

Aromatic Having a strong, pleasant smell.

Chapatis Round, flat Indian breads. The bread is unleavened, meaning it is not made to rise with yeast.

Charcoal A fuel made from wood that has been partly burnt to make black lumps or sticks.

Chilli A small, hot-tasting green or red pepper. It is often dried and ground to make a powder, and used as a spice.

Columbus, Christopher The Italian sailor and explorer who, in 1492, was the first European to reach America. Before this time, Europeans did not know that America existed.

Culture The art, history and traditions that make a society, or group of people, different from any other.

Curd A firm, creamy substance made from milk. Curd forms when the watery liquid in milk (the whey), separates from it.

Dams Barriers built across rivers to hold back the water.

Densely populated Having many people living close together.

Descendents The children, grandchildren, great-grandchildren, and so on, of people who lived in earlier times.

Dough A sticky paste made from flour and kneaded until it is very elastic. Bread is made from dough.

Drainage A system of drains (channels or pipes) used for taking away waste water and sewage.

Export To sell food or other goods to countries abroad.

Foothills The smaller hills that surround a range of high mountains.

45

Hindi   A language spoken by many people in India. It is one of the country's official languages.

Marinating   Soaking meat or fish in spices with oil, yogurt or wine, to make it tasty and tender.

Paddy fields   Fields flooded with water for growing rice.

Peninsular   A piece of land that sticks out into the sea and is almost completely surrounded by water.

Pestle and mortar   A special pounding tool and bowl used for grinding spices and other substances to a powder.

Plantations   Large areas of land which have been planted out with bushes or trees. Plantations are used for growing tea, cotton and rubber trees.

Poverty A serious lack of money that leads to a poor standard of living.

Pulses   The seeds of certain plants. Peas, beans and lentils are all pulses. They are often dried.

Relishes   Tasty sauces eaten with other foods to add extra flavour.

Sacred   Holy.

Semolina   The hard grains left after wheat or other cereals have been ground up to make flour.

Simmer   Boil gently.

Spices   Strong-tasting substances used to add flavour to food. They are often ground into a powder or paste.

Subcontinent   An area of land that is large, but smaller than a continent. The seven continents of the world are Europe, Asia, North and South America, Africa, Australia and Antarctica.

Temperate   Neither very hot nor very cold.

Traditions   The customs passed down by people over the centuries.

Tropical   A word which describes the very hot, wet climate of the tropics (the areas to the north and south of the Equator).

Vegetarians   People who do not eat meat.

Vermicelli   A kind of pasta made in very thin strands.

Yeast   A fungus that causes a chemical reaction, called fermentation, when it is added to food. Yeast makes dough rise to make bread.

46

Further information

Recipe books

The Cooking of Southern India by Rafi Fernandez (Sainsbury, 1992)

Madhur Jaffery's Indian Cookery by Madhur Jaffery (BBC Books, 1993)

A useful book, *The Flavours of Gujarat* (Virani, 1991), is available by mail order from Virani Food Products Ltd, 10-14 Stewarts Road, Finedon Road Industrial Estate, Wellingborough, Northants NN8 4RJ.

Information books

Focus on India by Shahrukh a Husani (Hamish Hamilton, 1986)

India (Countries of the World) by David Cumming (Wayland, 1989)

Inside India by Prodeepta Das (Franklin Watts, 1990)

Through the year in India by Carol and John Ogle (Batsford, 1983)

Acknowledgements

The publishers would like to thank the following for allowing their photographs to be reproduced: Anthony Blake Photo Library 20 top; Bridgeman Art Library 9 both; Cephas 26 (N. Blythe); Chapel Studios frontispiece, 11 bottom, 12 (J. Heinrich), 16, 18 top (T. Richardson), 22 top, 25 top, 27, 28 bottom, 30 top, 31, 34, 36, 38, 44; Bruce Coleman Ltd 6 (G. Cubitt), 8 top (G. Cubitt); Greg Evans International 13 top (G. Evans), 14 top (G. Roy), 15 bottom (R. Van Raders); Eye Ubiquitous 4 (C. Johnson), 7 top , 14 bottom (P. Field), 15 top (P. Bouineau), 18 bottom (P. Smith), 19 (C. Johnson), 22 bottom (D. Cumming), 23, 24 top, 25 bottom (P. Seheult), 29 (D. Cumming), 32, 40 (P. Seheult); Hutchison Library 27, 33 top (L. Taylor), 33 bottom (M. Saunders); Tony Stone Worldwide 7 bottom (H. Kavanagh), 10 top (S. and N. Geary), 20 bottom (J. Jackson), 28 top (D. Hanson), 30 bottom (C. Haigh); Wayland Picture Library cover inset (A. Blackburn); Zefa 8 bottom, 11 top (Reinhard), 24 bottom.

The map artwork on page 5 was supplied by Peter Bull. The recipe artwork on pages 17 and 35-44 was supplied by Judy Stevens.

The author would like to thank Meena Patak, of Patak Spices, and Mrs Sandy Samani. Also thanks to Tilda Rice and the Indian High Commission, London.

Index

America, foods from 11
Aryans, the 9

biriyani 13
Bombay 7, 30, 33
breads 26-7, 36-7
British Raj 11

Calcutta 7
chapatis 20, 22, 26-7
chay 18, 21, 30
chilli peppers 11, 24
Christians 13
chutney 11
crops 8, 14-16, 18
curry 11, 23

Deccan Plateau 7, 8
Delhi 7
desserts 31, 38-9
dhal 30
Diwali 33, 42
drinks 30

farming 14-16, 18
festivals 32-3
fish 13

Ganges, River 7

ghee 10, 33
Goa 13
Gujarat 13

Himalayas, the 6
Hindus 9, 10, 33

Id 33
India
  capital of 7
  climate in 7-8
  geography of 6-7
  history of 9-11
  map of 5
  population 4, 14
Indian Ocean 7
Indus, River 9

kedgeree 11, 34
kitchiri 34-5
korma 13

Madras 7
meal times 20-21
meat 10-11, 20
Moguls, the 9-10
monsoon, the 8
mountains 6-7
Muslims 9, 11, 13, 33

poppadums 21

pulses 15, 29-30

raitas 20, 21, 44
Rajasthan 12
Ramadan 33
religion 6, 9-11
rice 15-17, 42-3
rice pudding 11, 31, 38
rivers 7, 9

samosas 22
snack food 21-2
spices 11, 23-5, 29
sugar-cane 14-15, 30
sweets 21, 31

Taj Mahal, the 10
tandoori dishes 12, 40-41
tea 18, 30
tiffin boxes 21
tikka dishes 12

vegetables 28-9
vegetarianism 10, 13, 28, 29
vindaloo 13

weddings 32

yogurt 10, 30, 44